ART TELLS A STORY SERIES

Royal Persia
Tales and Art of Iran

BY CARELLA ALDEN

The Metropolitan Museum of Art
Rogers Fund, 1957

Based on the production in the
series for young people, Art Entertainments,
presented at The Metropolitan Museum of Art.

PARENTS' MAGAZINE PRESS • NEW YORK

Thomas, Richard and Charles

Library of Congress Cataloging in Publication Data

Alden, Carella.
  Royal Persia.

  (Art tells a story series)
  SUMMARY: Traces the history of the Persian Empire
with emphasis on the art and other aspects of its
culture.
  "Based on the production in the series for young
people, Art entertainments, presented at the Metropolitan
Museum of Art."
    1. Iran—History—Juvenile literature.   2. Art,
Iranian—Juvenile literature.   ·[1. Iran—History.
2. Art, Iranian]   I. Title.
DS273.A34   935'.05   72-1818
ISBN 0-8193-0610-X
ISBN 0-8193-0611-8 (lib. bdg.)

CONTENTS

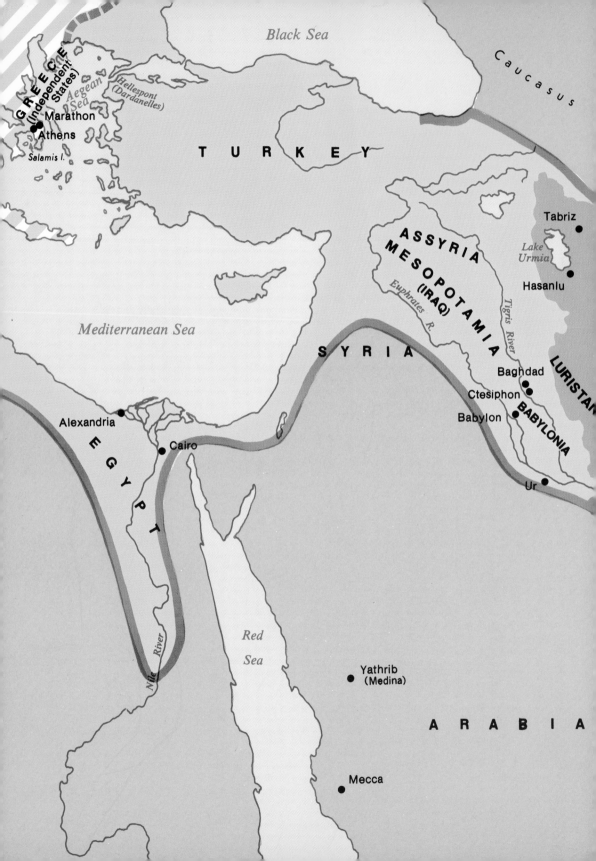

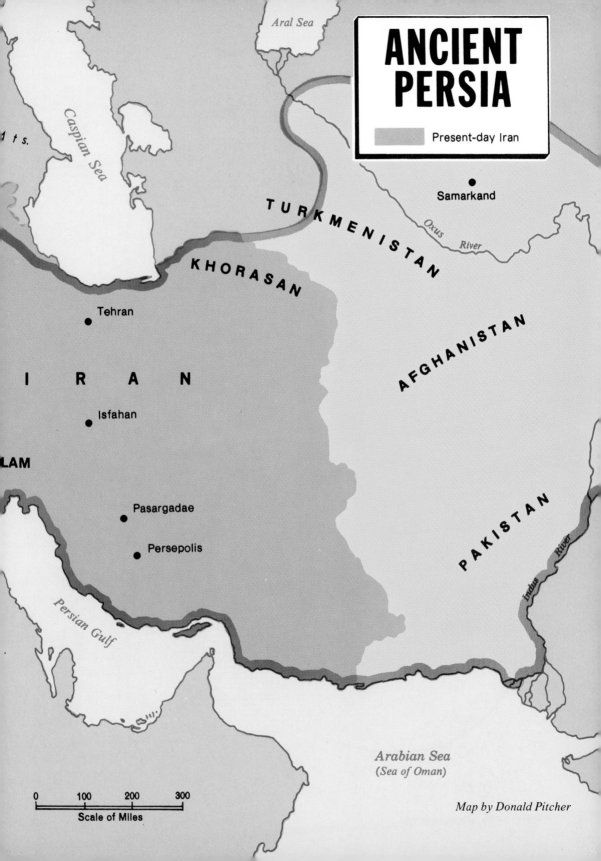

CHAPTER ONE

ARRIVAL

As you approach Tehran by airplane, you view a very modern city of the twentieth century. But later, as you fly to other places, you see the ruins of very ancient cities. They are now only mounds on the landscape, or walls and chambers exposed by the careful digging of archaeologists. One is the ancient city of Hasanlu, not far from Tabriz, which contains the remains of several

Courtesy of Douglas V. Waugh
Aerial view of Tehran, Iran

*People who lived in some of the buried settlements, like
Hasanlu, in Iran, knew of Abraham or Nebuchadnezzar and
Daniel because they lived during their lifetimes. We know
of them from the Bible.*

settlements, each built at different periods. What
archaeologists found at Hasanlu tells the fate of two of
the ancient settlements and of the people who lived
in them.

In one, very little remained except the walls of houses.
It is highly possible that the people who lived there heard
rumors of an invading enemy moving toward their city.
And so, having time, they packed up all their possessions
and moved on.

The people who lived at an earlier time, in the settlement beneath, were not as fortunate. One day, in the fall of the year, an enemy suddenly stole up on them and threw lighted torches into their mud-brick houses. Panic broke out. It all happened so quickly only a few could have escaped. Many were burned to death. Others were killed when walls and ceilings crashed down on them. This debris became their tomb. As time passed, winds blew dirt and grasses into the wreckage and rains helped pack them down. Eventually the later tribe moved into the valley and built their settlement on top of the buried one. There they lived until that day when they heard about their danger and moved on to safety.

In the 1950s, teams of archaeologists from the University of Pennsylvania and The Metropolitan Museum

Courtesy of Oscar Muscarella

An archaeologist from the University Museum and two Iranian assistants examine a skeleton at Hasanlu. The skeleton lies on its stomach. With it are objects made of copper and bronze.

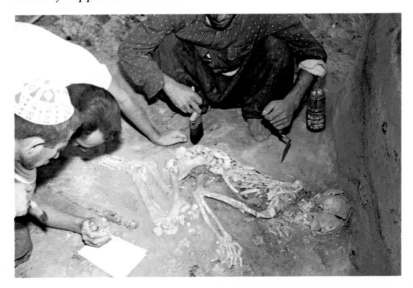

The objects found on the skeleton were cleaned and found to be
brooches, or clasps, in the shape of lions, dating from
the 9th century B.C. Behind them were pins to fasten to clothing.
It is not known what the chain was used for.

of Art began digging at Hasanlu. They soon discovered it
was not the site of just one settlement but of several. In
one was the grim evidence of mass deaths. Skeletons of
men, women, and children were in positions of fright and
panic. Charred walls and household goods revealed death
and destruction by fire. The archaeologists also knew
these people were not a primitive tribe. Scattered all
around were luxury items, and some of the skeletons still
wore jewelry. From the kinds of charred crops found, the
archaeologists knew the tragedy took place during harvest
time, in the fall. And how long ago did it happen?

Scientific tests showed it was in the late ninth century B.C., about 2,850 years ago.

As the airplane engines hum on, carrying you toward Tabriz, you realize that that was some three hundred years before the founding of the mighty Persian Empire.

The Metropolitan Museum of Art
Gift of Mrs. Constantine Sidamon-Eristoff, 1961

One of a pair of bronze handles in the shape of a bird found at Hasanlu. Before cleaning and after cleaning.

*This chapter is based on an article by Oscar Muscarella in the November 1966 *Bulletin* of The Metropolitan Museum of Art.

CHAPTER TWO

KING OF KINGS

I am Cyrus, king of the universe, great king, mighty king, king of lands."

So proclaimed Cyrus to the people after conquering Babylon in 539 B.C. This last great victory of the "king of kings" completed the empire he had founded. It extended from the Indus River, in what is now Pakistan, to the Mediterranean Sea, and from the Caucasus Mountains to the Indian Ocean.

Cyrus was a member of a Persian clan known as the Achaemenids. They in turn were members of a tribe called Pasargadae. Cyrus built a city and named it Pasargadae in honor of his tribe. It was his capital.

A particular name has been given to the period in which the first great Persian kings ruled. It is called Achaemenid.

When Cyrus died his son Cambyses ruled. He conquered Egypt for the empire.

The third great king of kings was Darius I who extended the empire into India. He secured all the borders and placed governors in the provinces. He built roads and waterways as a system of communication for all his lands. Like Cyrus, Darius was a fine statesman and a just ruler who permitted all peoples to worship as they chose.

Traveling by car across a high plain rimmed by stone mountains, you come upon the remains of what was one of the greatest architectural structures in the ancient world. It is Persepolis, "City of Persia," founded by Darius in 518 B.C. Its size alone is impressive. Among its most handsome features were the stone columns. Row after row of them supported wooden roofs. Sculpture also added to the beauty and grandeur.

Courtesy of Vaughn E. Crawford

The remains of the palaces of Darius and Xerxes can still be seen at Persepolis. There was also a harem, the house where the many royal wives lived; a treasury; a throne room, called The Hall of 100 Columns; and a large audience hall. Here, in the center, you see the reconstructed harem.

*This sculpture represents a legendary royal bird of Persia.
It is said the ancient Persians believed that if the bird's
shadow fell on a man, that man would become a king.*

*A lion attacking a bull is carved in relief
on the outer walls of a number
of stairways at Persepolis.*

Courtesy of The Oriental Institute, University of Chicago

*Each year, from all over the empire, tribute was brought to
the king—gold, jewels, silks, carpets, and other works of art.*

The University Museum, University of Pennsylvania
Perrot and Chipiez, Histoire de l'Art, *vol. V pl. IX*

*This is an archaeologist's drawing of the palace of
Darius as it may have looked in ancient times. Far
to the right is a rock-cliff tomb.*

Persepolis was a ceremonial center used only for very special occasions. The most important one was the annual spring festival. Persepolis was also a symbol of the Persian Empire, for only an empire of such wealth and power could have created it.

After building Persepolis, Darius tried to conquer Greece, but his army was defeated at the battle of Marathon.

Upon the death of Darius, his son Xerxes became king. He too was an able administrator, but the defeat of the Persians at Marathon made him vengeful. Gathering a huge army and navy from all over his empire he planned a second invasion of Greece. His forces met at the Hellespont (now the Dardanelles in Turkey). It took seven days and seven nights for Xerxes's army of 1,700,000 men to cross the narrow water lane.

The Metropolitan Museum of Art Harris Brisbane Dick Fund, 1954

Before crossing to Greece, on history's first pontoon bridge, Xerxes poured wine from a gold cup into the Hellespont as an offering. The cup may have looked like this one made in the 5th century B.C.

Once in Greece, Xerxes was victorious. Hearing of these victories the people of Athens fled from their city. When the Persians reached there they found it deserted. With no one to do battle against they burned the city of Athens. The Persians were finally defeated in a great sea battle at Salamis, and Xerxes returned to Persia.

One hundred and fifty years later, Alexander the Great conquered the Persian Empire. When he came upon Persepolis, he was so awed by its beauty that he remained there several months. It is believed that just before leaving, his troops burned Persepolis out of revenge for the Persians' having burned Athens.

But enough of Persepolis remains to give us an understanding of the beauty and magnitude of the Persian Empire in the days of the mighty kings.

Courtesy of The Oriental Institute, University of Chicago

King Darius is shown receiving a dignitary.

CHAPTER THREE

A NEW SPLENDOR

The conquest of Persia by Alexander the Great was the first of many conquests that were to follow. But after each one an interesting thing happened. In a sense, the conquerors became the conquered. Like Alexander, they fell in love with Persia. They learned the Persian language, took to wearing Persian dress, adopted Persian manners, and married Persian women. Alexander married a princess named Roxana.

Alexander was one of history's greatest military leaders, but when he died, at age 33, he left no real organization to hold together the vast empire he had conquered. Because of this, the Greek occupation of Persia was weak.

Taking advantage of this weakness, a tribe from northeast Iran forced the Greeks out and began building an empire of their own. They were the Parthians.

For over four hundred years the Parthians were the rulers of Persia. But their administrators, scholars, engineers, scientists, and artists were Persian.

In this 16th-century painting, the artist has pictured Alexander in Persian dress, in a completely Persian setting.

Once, this 4th-century helmet glistened in the sunlight. The bands of bronze were highly polished, as were the sheets of patterned silver covering the sections of iron. The lining was of leather. It was probably worn by a Sasanian chieftain or king.

As time passed, the Parthians permitted the rise of great Persian landowners who were expert cavalrymen equipped with fine armor. They also had soldiers to help protect their lands from raiding tribes. Eventually they became very powerful and began to rebel against the Parthians.

One day the chief of a Persian province, named Ardeshir, took up arms against the Parthian king and in the year 226 killed him in single combat. Ardeshir came from a noble family, the Sasanid, who were descendants of the Achaemenids. Ardeshir began the Sasanian dynasty and, under it, all Persia reawakened to the glory of Achaemenian times.

New palaces were built, including a magnificent one in their capital at Ctesiphon on the Tigris River. Fortresses rose and, because there was a revival of the ancient religion that worshiped Ahura Mazda, the god of light, fire temples were built. Persia, the land between East and West, grew rich again and this wealth invited conquest.

Ahura Mazda was the Persian god of light. The disk perhaps represents the sun, for the sun was the symbol of ancient Persia. The carving is at Persepolis.

The Roman Emperor Valerian, his hands in chains, kneels before the Persian King, Shapur I, who is seated on his horse.

In the West, Roman emperors had looked eastward for many years, but each time their legions attacked they were held back. In one such battle, the Sasanians were led by their new king of kings, Shapur I, the son of Ardeshir. Leading the Romans was their emperor, Valerian. Valerian was captured by Shapur and taken prisoner. To commemorate this victory, the Persians had a large relief sculpture cut into a cliff near Persepolis.

Courtesy of The Smithsonian Institution,
Freer Gallery of Art, Washington, D.C.

A scene of Shapur II hunting decorates this 4th-century plate.
So much fine art was made in Sasanian times that it was used
not only in the Near East but also in Europe and China.

Hunting was a popular sport in Persia and a hunting
scene on a silver-gilt plate was a challenge to the
silversmith.

One of the rarest objects of Persian art is a silver
sculpture of the head of a Sasanian king. Just which king
he represents remains a mystery. Whoever created it was
a superb craftsman. Whoever ordered it must have taken
great pride in the art and culture of the Sasanian dynasty,
which lasted for four hundred years. It would be a
long time before Persia would see such splendor again.

One cannot help but notice the unusual crowns worn by the
Sasanian kings. Each differed a little from the other, but
all were topped with a ball. The meaning of the ball is
not known.

CHAPTER FOUR

FROM OUT OF A DESERT

Across the Persian Gulf lay the land of Arabia. Its most important town during the sixth century was Mecca. About 570, a boy was born there and named Mohammed. His father died before he was born, his mother when he was six. He was raised by an uncle and, like many boys in Arabia, he tended sheep. When he grew up he became a merchant. In his travels he came in contact with many Jews and Christians. From them, Mohammed learned of their one God.

One day Mohammed had a dream. The angel Gabriel spoke to him and told him he was to be the apostle of God and prophet to his people. In Mecca he began preaching of the one God. His name in Arabic is Allah. The name of the religion is Islam and one who believes is a Muslim, "one who submits." Mohammed's teachings were first memorized by his students. Later on they were

Artists usually did not paint the face of Mohammed for fear of being sacrilegious, so they covered his face. The flame-shaped halo shows Mohammed is a holy man.

Arabic was the language used for writing the Koran. The earliest style of calligraphy, or writing, is called Kufic. This is a page from a 9th-century Kufic Koran.

put into writing in the Arabic language, and these writings comprise the Koran, the Bible of the Muslims.

Word of Mohammed and his teachings swept through the desert like the miracle of a rainstorm sweeping across the dry sand. Warring tribes became united under the banner of Islam. The poor now hungered for Mohammed's faith. But the rich, especially in Mecca, condemned him, for they feared his power.

In 622 Mohammed and his followers left Mecca and went to the city of Yathrib which became known as Medina, "city of the Prophet." This exit is called the Hegira, "the Flight."

The wealthy of Mecca finally accepted Islam as the "true faith" and Mohammed returned to make the city the spiritual center of Islam. Medina remained its political center. Ever since, a pilgrimage to Mecca, at least once in a lifetime, is required of every Muslim.

After Mohammed's death, Arab Muslims on horseback, in camel caravans, and on foot, swept out of the Arabian

"Prayer in the Mosque." Oil painting by Jean Léon Gérôme (1824-1904)

The Muslim house of worship is called a mosque. Its design was based on Mohammed's home in Medina, which was an arrangement of small huts around a courtyard.

Here, the man in the foreground stands on his own prayer rug. Worshippers face a prayer niche in a wall called a mihrab. It indicates the direction of Mecca.

deserts brandishing scimitars (curved swords) and carrying the Koran. They conquered not just by the sword alone but by their faith. They asked no man his native tribe nor did they notice the color of his skin. They asked him only to believe "There is no god but Allah, and Mohammed is His Prophet."

The Metropolitan Museum of Art
Bequest of Catherine Lorillard Wolfe, 1887
"Arabs Crossing a Ford." Oil on wood by Eugène Fromentin (1820-1876)

CHAPTER FIVE

CITY ON THE TIGRIS

About 651, the Persians were conquered by the Arabs who ruled Persia for six hundred years.

Arab rulers, called caliphs, established their capital at a city named Baghdad, in the land known then as Mesopotamia and now called Iraq. Baghdad, on the Tigris River, was one of the oldest cities in the Middle East. To create the new capital, the first caliph, the

Courtesy of Andrea Rawle
Photograph: Philip Evola
Illustration by Edmund Dulac
for "The Sleeper Awakened"
from The Arabian Nights
(London, Hodder and Stoughton)

Baghdad on the Tigris River

spiritual head of Islam, ordered the finest architects and craftsmen from all over the empire to come to Baghdad. Many came from Persia. When completed, the capital formed a circle two miles across. It was called "the round city," its shape probably inspired by Persian cities of the time. In the very center rose the caliph's marble palace with a golden dome.

Merchants arrived at Baghdad, their camels laden with goods from the East and the West. From this trade the world of Islam grew rich and the fountain from which its wealth poured was Baghdad. Baghdad also became the center for scholars, astronomers, scientists of all kinds, and for artists and writers.

At the time of Charles the Great (Charlemagne), Haroun al-Rashid became caliph at Baghdad in 786. He was a scholar and poet and a patron of the arts. To his palace came musicians and storytellers to entertain him.

From earliest times, the most popular form of entertainment was story telling, and professional storytellers roamed their small world relating tales of wonder. But by the time of Haroun al-Rashid, the world was much larger and the men of the caravans, and of the sea, were returning from the East not only with merchandise but with marvelous tales. Over the years, the stories spread all through the world of Islam, but they were never written down. Most people could not read and the scribes and poets did not think the tales worth bothering about.

Just when, and where, and by whom, the tales were

Here, two gentlemen listen to poetry just as Haroun
al-Rashid did in his palace at Baghdad. In the center
is a fountain. Now and then, a musician softly strikes
a tambourine.

"The Enchanted Horse" by Edmond Dulac (1882-1953) for The Arabian Nights. *Photograph: Philip Evola from the original watercolor in a private collection.*

"It was dark and the Prince of Persia could see nothing. He was obliged to allow the horse to direct his own course."
Dulac was a gifted illustrator early in this century. His watercolor illustrations for The Arabian Nights *were exhibited in London in 1907.*

finally put into Arabic script is not known. But in 1704, in Paris, four volumes of the tales appeared translated into French by an archaeologist named Antoine Galland. Their title was, *Les Mille et Une Nuit (The Thousand and One Nights).* We know them best as *The Arabian Nights.*

The heroine of the stories is named Scheherazade, a daughter of the vizier, a high government official, who lived in Baghdad and told stories to the Sultan, the king, for a thousand and one nights to keep him from killing her. Her cleverness lay in never ending a story in one evening. Instead, she always managed to be in the middle of the tale so he would let her live another day to learn how the story came out.

Scheherazade is supposed to have lived in Baghdad during the reign of Haroun al-Rashid.

Haroun al-Rashid, with his brilliant vizier, gave Baghdad its most enlightened period and, during his reign, he and Charlemagne exchanged gifts, addressing each other as "Master of the East" and "Master of the West."

Courtesy of Andrea Rawle
Photograph: Philip Evola
"Scheherazade" by Edmond
Dulac from The Thousand and One
Nights *(Paris, Edition d'Art*
H. Piazza)

Scheherazade

CHAPTER SIX

GARDEN ON A CARPET

C arpet-making is one of the oldest crafts in the world.
It is also one of the earliest ways in which man
expressed his creative talent for design and color. In
Persia carpet-making became almost a symbol of the land.
When Alexander visited the tomb of Cyrus, he marveled
at the beautiful carpets on which stood the gold funeral
couch of the king of kings. By late Sasanian times, Persian

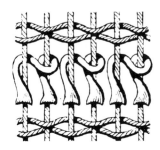

Courtesy of Hanna Erdmann
Reproduced from Oriental Carpets
(New York, 1962) by Kurt Erdmann

The Senneh knot used by
Persian weavers is often
called the Persian knot.

Courtesy of Vaughn E. Crawford

The tomb of King Cyrus
at Pasargadae, Iran.

Photograph: Hans Namuth

The ancient Persian art of rug-making has been handed down from generation to generation. Once upon a time the patterns were memorized; now they are usually drawn on paper for the weaver to follow while knotting the woolen threads. This Iranian artist holds a knife for cutting the loops of wool that make the soft pile finish.

carpets were famous throughout the Middle East and as far away as China. Over the "silk route" the finest were sent by caravan as gifts to the emperor.

In Persia much of the land is dry, so water has always been very precious. Therefore a garden of flowers nourished by a bubbling fountain or quiet pool was a great luxury. Poets wrote of their beauty, painters painted them. To Persians, Paradise is a magnificent garden. So much did gardens mean to the people of Persia that one of the most popular designs for carpets was a garden pattern.

In the audience hall of the Sasanian capital at Ctesiphon, not far from Baghdad, was once the most costly carpet ever made. It is known in history as the Spring or Winter carpet of Khusraw. Its design was a formal garden. But what a garden! Flowers, birds, trees, and a stream were all created of gleaming precious jewels. The border around the carpet represented the green fields beyond the garden. It was a solid mass of emeralds.

This carpet represented more than the wealth of the empire. It had a religious meaning as well. It stood for spring when all life is renewed, and for Paradise, the reward for earthly struggle. In winter, it was a reminder of both.

The Metropolitan Museum of Art
Gift of Alexander Smith Cochran, 1913

As nymphs bathe in the pool of this "garden paradise," a girl dances to music played on a harp.

During the wave of Arab conquest, the marble palace at Ctesiphon was ransacked. The famous Spring-Winter carpet became the booty of the invaders. But for a long time it was the inspiration for other formal garden carpets.

Private collection of Joseph V. McMullan
Photograph: Otto E. Nelson
Period of Shah Abbas I (reigned 1587-1629)

There is a pool in the center of this formal garden carpet. Two waterways flow out from the pool. Find the blue and the white fish and the water plants in the streams. Flowering bushes are in the garden. The pointed star shapes in each corner may represent tents. Stylized leaves surround the carpet.

CHAPTER SEVEN

DECORATION

Among the contributions the Arabs gave to the world were their language, their literature, and the science of mathematics. But their finest art came from the lands they conquered. Today, the art of those lands is called Islamic art.

Islamic art was often designed not only to be beautiful but to also express the religious faith of Islam. Words from the Koran are on many of the objects, and sometimes just Arabic letters were used purely as abstract design. Islamic craftsmen also enjoyed doing all-over decoration. They decorated their objects with unending variations of curving lines and geometric patterns interlaced with the graceful Arabic writing.

No longer were the silversmith and goldsmith the most important craftsmen as they had been in earlier times. Now it was the potter, the glassmaker, the metalworker, the carver of wood and ivory.

The Metropolitan Museum of Art
Pfeiffer Fund, 1964

This 10th-century ivory elephant is a chess piece. The game of chess is believed to have originated in India, then spread to Persia.

The Metropolitan Museum of Art
Edward C. Moore Collection
Bequest of Edward C. Moore, 1891

Mosque lamps were often made of glass and decorated with gilt and enamel colors. Chains or cords were pulled through the loops to hang the lamp. You can see lamps hanging in the picture on page 27.

The Metropolitan Museum of Art
Rogers Fund, 1957

One of the most popular Sasanian kings was named Bahram Gur. His adventures were often described in stories and art. He loved a beautiful slave girl named Azadeh, who played the harp. Bahram Gur often took Azadeh with him on hunting trips. This 12th-century painted and glazed pottery bowl shows the famous couple seated on a camel.

The Metropolitan Museum of Art
Rogers Fund, 1951

Incense was often used in Persian palaces. Craftsmen created incense burners to be attractive as well as practical. This one, of bronze, was made with open-work decoration that allowed the sweet-smelling smoke to escape from the burner.

The Metropolitan Museum of Art
Rogers Fund, 1910

Carved flowers, foliage, and Arabic writing decorate this wooden Koran stand. The Tree of Life, a design often used in art of the Middle East, is framed in an archway near the bottom.

CHAPTER EIGHT

PAINTERS OF STORIES

Persian painters were artists of book illustration. The earliest ones designed the space in their pictures on a "single plane." One looks at the picture at eye level. Later painters used an arrangement called "high horizon." One sees the picture as if looking down at it from above. Persian painters rarely concerned themselves with western-type perspective. Instead, they chose to show everything to its best advantage.

*The Metropolitan Museum of Art
Rogers Fund, 1913*

This page from a manuscript shows a doctor preparing a cough medicine. It is a "single plane" picture painted in the 13th century.

This picture, painted about 1524, is an example of "high horizon." The artist shows us a court scene. King Khusraw is seated on his throne. Members of his court seem to be busy among themselves. The king looks very lonely. A carpet, cut at the corners, is used as a canopy for the throne.

This picture seems to illustrate
Sa'di's verse very well!

A Persian poet named Sa'di wrote:
> *However much you study, you cannot*
> *know without action.*
> *A donkey laden with books is neither*
> *an intellectual nor a wise man.*
> *Empty of essence, what learning has he—*
> *Whether upon him is firewood or book?*

The greatest Persian story was completed in 1011. It is called the Shah-nameh or Book of Kings. Its author's name was Firdausi, and the hero of many exciting adventures in it is named Rustam.

The finest painters in Persia were commissioned by kings and princes to illustrate the Shah-nameh. Then many years later these beautiful books, for one reason or another, were sold. They were usually taken apart and the paintings sold in groups or even separately. Fortunately, many are now in museums all over the world where people can enjoy looking at them.

Private collection of Arthur A. Houghton, Jr.
Photograph: William F. Pons

Here we see Rustam slaying a dragon with the help of his wonderful and fearless horse, Rakhsh. The painting is from the Shah-nameh made for Shah Tahmasp.

This 12th-century Persian sculpture shows the face of a Mongol-type man. He wears a peaked cap.

About 1225, Mongol hordes, from across the wastelands of Russia, had invaded the world of Islam. Led by their chieftain, Genghis Khan, wave after wave swept through Persia and neighboring lands. They killed thousands of people and destroyed many cities. Later, Tamerlane, a Turk, led the ruthless destruction of Baghdad. Yet all through that dark period, the art and literature produced are proof that the spirit of the people was never conquered.

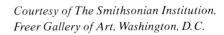

A 17th-century Persian painter at work.

The Metropolitan Museum of Art
Rogers Fund, 1955

Tamerlane is pictured here in war dress. His horse is clad in plate armor. Persian painters often illustrated armies by showing only the soldiers' heads behind mountains.

CHAPTER NINE

HALF THE WORLD

In 1499 a courageous warrior, who had won victory over
the Turks in western Persia, crowned himself Shah, or
king. Persian kings sometimes crowned themselves. All
Persia rejoiced, for this warrior, Ismail by name, claimed
royal lineage back through the Sasanian dynasty to the
Achaemenean kings. He was truly a king of kings. From
a distinguished member of his family came the name of
the dynasty he founded, Safavid.

The greatest and most famous of the Safavid rulers
came to the throne in 1587. He was Shah Abbas I and is
rightfully called the Great. His long reign was a period of
progress unequaled since the kings of old. On the site of
an ancient city, named Isfahan, he built his capital. Today,
as it did then, it represents the finest examples of
Persian architecture.

As you approach Isfahan by airplane, you think of it as
an oasis. Around the city is desert and to the south rise
bleak mountains. But the patches of blue you see from the
air are not water holes. They are the blue tile domes of
mosques appearing like jewels in the sunlight.

Dome of Madresseh-e Chahar Bagh,
a religious school in Isfahan, Iran.

Vaulted domes and arches had long been a popular
form of construction in Persia. But it was the art of the
potter that brought the crowning splendor to the
architects' grand design.

Just as the people of Europe built cathedrals in which
to worship God, the people of Islam built mosques in
which to worship Allah.

Courtesy of Iran Air

The great square in Isfahan.

Shah Abbas, with his master architect, planned his
capital around a huge square. The buildings that surround
it dazzle your eyes with their color and stir your
imagination. In the center of the square, today, is a
fountain splashing water into a pool. Sitting down at the
edge of the pool you close your eyes and imagine the
scene as you know it once was. There is no longer a pool
or paved roads. The great square is the Maidan-e Shah,

the playground of the Shah. Now it is a polo field and the finest players, members of the Shah's court and army, are challenging each other. All around the "maidan" the people of Isfahan watch and cheer their favorite player when he gives the ball an especially good strike. From a

The Metropolitan Museum of Art
Hewitt Fund, 1911.
Detail from a manuscript painting, "A Polo Game" (16th century).

In the foreground of the picture you can see goal posts. The goal posts used during the royal polo games still stand today in the great square at Isfahan.

balcony of his palace, Shah Abbas, clothed in a robe of rich brocade and wearing a turban crowned with jewels, watches the game. When it ends he presents a handsome gold cup to the winner.

Courtesy of Vaughn E. Crawford

Ali Qapu, the palace of Shah Abbas I.

The heat of the sun wakes you from your daydream of the past. You rise and leave the square to view, at close range, the buildings that are among the architectural masterpieces of the world.

Courtesy of Vaughn E. Crawford

Entrance to the Royal Mosque, Masjid-e Shah. It was ordered by Shah Abbas I and is the largest mosque built during the Safavid period. From its towers, called minarets, muezzins called the faithful to prayer.

Courtesy of Vaughn E. Crawford

Inside the Masjid-e Shah Mosque.

Everywhere are domes and the color blue. Light blue, green-blue, purple-blue, dark blue. Here and there is yellow. The sky is blue and the sun is yellow. Could the shapes and colors represent the dome of heaven?

In the time of Shah Abbas, the people said of their capital, "Isfahan is half the world," meaning in importance and beauty. As you leave Isfahan you say to yourself, "It is still half the world in beauty."

Courtesy of Vaughn E. Crawford

Detail of entrance to the Masjid-e Sh⌐¹ ˙˙

CHAPTER TEN

DEPARTURE

Early in the eighteenth century the last rich period of Persian art ended. Other dynasties rose and fell; periodically invaders swept across the land, and the capital was moved from beautiful Isfahan to a dusty little village named Tehran.

In 1925 a new dynasty began named Pahlavi. Its founder's name was Reza. Reza Shah was aware that Persia had a long way to go in order to move into the twentieth century, but he began the struggle. In order to have the world relate to the rebirth in his country, he decreed, in 1935, that henceforward Persia would be known as Iran.

The name Iran comes from the name Aryan. The Aryans were a group of wandering tribes that migrated into Iran in very ancient times. The name Persia was given to the land by the Greeks. They took it from Parsa, the name of the region from which the first great kings came.

In 1941, Reza Shah's son became king. He bore the

Courtesy of Iran Air

Their Imperial Majesties, Shahanshah Aryamehr and Empress Farah at their coronation in 1967.

same name as his father. Twenty-two-year-old Reza Shah was handsome, well educated, intelligent, and ambitious for Iran. But he refused to crown himself king. It is said his reason was that he did not wish to be "ruler of a nation of beggars." By 1961 Reza Shah began sweeping reforms.

In October 1967 his coronation took place. He was no longer ruler of a "nation of beggars."

In October 1971, by royal invitation, rulers and dignitaries from around the world assembled on the ancient grounds of Persepolis and Pasargadae to celebrate, with the Shah and his people, the 2,500th anniversary of

Courtesy of Robert H. Dyson, Jr.

During Iran's 2,500th anniversary, floats bearing ancient ships passed in a parade that recalled the great periods of Persia's long history.

the founding of the Persian Empire by Cyrus the Great, King of Kings. In only ten years, Pahlavi (Reza Shah) had thrust his country from a backward nation to one of the most influential in the Middle East.

The Shah has said, "Today my country is a show window of the blend of ancient and modern."

As you arrive at the airport in Tehran it is dusk. When you board the airplane you notice a figure on the tailwing. The image is familiar; somewhere you have seen it before. Of course, it's the head of the legendary royal bird you saw at Persepolis. After 2,500 years he has finally taken to flight.

Courtesy of Iran Air

When you are airborne you settle back and close your eyes and relax. Suddenly you are not flying in an airplane at all. You are on a magic carpet and the carpet is a garden. You open your eyes to look up at the sky. Millions of stars are shining. Then, as the airplane banks to head on its course, the sky appears to form a dome over the earth. And the dome is a deep blue studded with stars. It is a dome over royal Persia.

Celestial photograph: Robert T. Little

PRONUNCIATION GUIDE

Capital letters indicate the part of the word that is stressed most. Persian
words are pronounced evenly unless they have been anglicized. The sound of
the Persian "h" is unlike any sound we use in speaking. It is breathy and formed
at the back of the throat. If the sound were "spelled," it might be "hock."

Abbas	ah-bahs
Abbasid	ah-bah-sid
Achaemenian	aka-MEAN-ee-an
Achaemenid	a-KEM-e-nid
Ahura Mazda	a-hura maz-da
Ali Qapu	ah-lee cah-poo
Allah	al-lah
Antoine Galland	AN-twan gel-LAN
Archaeologist	are-key-OL-oh-gist
Ardeshir	are-de-sheer
Aryamehr	are-ya-mar
Aryan	ARE-ee-an
Azadeh	ah-zah-day
Baghdad	BAG-dad
Bahram Gur	bah-ram goor
Caliph	KAY-lif
Calligraphy	cal-LIG-ra-fee
Cambyses	cam-BY-seez
Charlemagne	SHAR-le-main
Ctesiphon	TES-i-fon
Caucasus	CAU-kah-suss
Cyrus	SY-russ
Dardanelles	dar-dan-ELZ
Debris	day-BREE
Delhi	DEL-ee
Firdausi	fair-dow-see
Genghis Khan	gen-ge-SKHAN
Haroun al-Rashid	hah-roon al-rash-eed
Hasanlu	hah-san-loo
Hegira	hedge-ira
Hellespont	HELL-es-pont
Indus	IN-duss
Iran	ear-RON
Iraq	ear-RACK
Isfahan	iss-fah-HAHN
Islam	iss-LAHM

Ismail	iss-mah-EEL
Khusraw	khoos-row
Koran	koe-RAN
Kufic	KOO-fik
Les Mille et Une Nuit	lay-meal ay oon-we
Madresseh-e Chahar Bagh	mad-reh-say-ay sha-har boch
Maidan-e Shah	may-dan-ay shah
Masjid-e Shah	mass-jed-ay shah
Medina	meh-DEE-nah
Mediterranean	med-i-ter-RAY-nee-an
Mesopotamia	mess-oh-poe-TAY-mia
Mihrab	meeh-rab
Mohammed	mo-HAM-ed
Mongol	MAHN-goal
Mosque	mahsk
Muezzins	moo-AY-zins
Mughals	MOO-galls
Muslim	MUZ-lim
Nebuchadnezzar	neb-oo-cod-NEZ-er
Nizami	nee-zah-me
Pahlavi	PAH-la-vee
Pakistan	pack-i-STAN
Parsa	PAR-sah
Parthians	PAR-thee-ans
Pasargadae	pah-SAR-ga-dee
Persepolis	per-SEP-eh-lis
Rokhsh	rock-sh
Reza	ray-zah
Rustam	ruh-stam
Sa'di	sah-dee
Safavid	saf-ah-vid
Salamis	SAL-eh-miss
Sasanian	sa-SAY-nee-an
Sasanid	SASS-ah-nid
Senneh	senna
Shahanshah	shah-an-shah
Shah-nameh	shah-nah-may
Shapur	sha-poor
Scheherazade	sheh-hair-ah-ZAHD
Tabriz	tah-BREEZE
Tahmasp	tah-mahsp
Tamerlane	TAM-er-lane
Tehran	tare-RON
Tigris	TIE-gris
Valerian	va-LER-ee-an
Vizier	veh-ZEER
Xerxes	ZERK-zees

INDEX

Figures in bold face indicate illustrations